EASY-TO-MAKE
CANDLES

GARY V. GUY

Photographs by
DAVE PEDEGANA

Second revised edition

DOVER PUBLICATIONS, INC.
NEW YORK

Publisher's Note

The publisher wishes to thank Dolores and Richard J. Scuderi of the Walnut Hill Company, P.O. Box 599, Bristol, Pennsylvania 19007, who aided in the publication of this second revised edition of *Easy-to-Make Candles*.

Since the original publication of this book, acrylic and plastic moulds have become popular in candlemaking. Instructions for their use are included on pp. 33-34.

Published in Canada by General Publishing Company, Ltd., 30 Lesmill Road, Don Mills, Toronto, Ontario.
Published in the United Kingdom by Constable and Company, Ltd.

This Dover edition, first published in 1979, is a revised republication of the work originally published in 1974 by Sterling Publishing Co., Inc., under the title *Tall Book of Candle Crafting*. Some of the color photographs from the original edition have been reproduced here on the covers. The Dover edition is published by special arrangement with Sterling Publishing Co., Inc., 2 Park Ave. New York, N.Y. 10016

International Standard Book Number: 0-486-23881-4
Library of Congress Catalog Card Number: 79-52768

Manufactured in the United States of America
Dover Publications, Inc.
31 East 2nd Street
Mineola, N.Y. 11501

Contents

Before You Begin

One would be hard put to find a person that does not enjoy an attractive, cleanly burning candle. The soft, soothing glow of a candle provides welcome relief from the harsh glare of electric bulbs and sickly light of fluorescent tubes. And a well-made, artistically shaped and colored candle pleasantly complements any room.

Even the most elaborate candles are remarkably simple to make—the ability to boil water is the only prerequisite for candle-making. Very few materials are required. All you really need for candle-making is wax, stearic acid (available in any craft shop), dye, a wick, and a few common household items. No special workshop is required either. You can work anywhere, as long as there is something to boil water with nearby.

The expense of candle-making, in keeping with the materials and tools required, is very low. After you become proficient at making candles you can even offset the cost by selling them. All the details needed to make candles as good as those turned out by professionals are in this book.

But enough introduction—on to candle-making! First, make a few simple block candles to get the feel of candle-making. Once you have mastered the basic techniques, you can easily make the most complicated-looking candle in this book. *Note:* If you have any confusion about wicks, dyes, waxes or moulds, just refer to the closing chapters of the book (pages 33–38), where these materials are completely explained. If your candles don't come out perfectly, and you can't find any reason for the imperfection, see the section on trouble-shooting at the end of the book. If you don't understand a term, see the glossary on page 40.

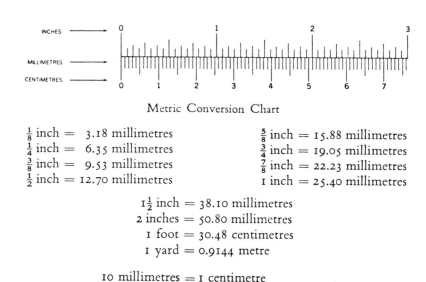

Metric Conversion Chart

$\frac{1}{8}$ inch = 3.18 millimetres $\frac{5}{8}$ inch = 15.88 millimetres
$\frac{1}{4}$ inch = 6.35 millimetres $\frac{3}{4}$ inch = 19.05 millimetres
$\frac{3}{8}$ inch = 9.53 millimetres $\frac{7}{8}$ inch = 22.23 millimetres
$\frac{1}{2}$ inch = 12.70 millimetres   1 inch = 25.40 millimetres

$1\frac{1}{2}$ inch = 38.10 millimetres
2 inches = 50.80 millimetres
1 foot = 30.48 centimetres
1 yard = 0.9144 metre

10 millimetres = 1 centimetre

1

Block Candles

The Basic Block Candle

Block candles are any large candles made with a mould. They are fast and easy to make and can be varied to suit your taste.

To make a block candle you need: a metal mould; one yard of medium-size wicking (if you make a candle where the wick must be inserted, use wire core wicking; otherwise, braided wicking is satisfactory); several pounds of 145° F. (63° C.) melting point wax (wax is designated by the temperature at which it melts); various colors of dye chips; scent (if desired); a candy, candle, or deep-fat thermometer; a few large tin cans or seamless coffee pots to melt the wax in; a few ounces of stearic acid; mould release; a pan to hold the water that will be heated; a flat bottom plastic or metal container with sides at least 10 inches high; and finally, an oven mitt for holding the hot containers of wax (Illus. 1).

Add water to the pan and place it on a burner to heat. Break up a few pounds of wax and place it in the pot or tin can. After the water has come to a boil, set the can of wax in it. A rack should be placed in the pan of water to keep the wax pot from touching the bottom of the double boiler. You need never worry about overheating the wax when using this double-boiler method as the wax will never reach a temperature beyond boiling. However, you must be careful that all the water does not boil away.

String the wick through the bottom hole of the mould, sealing it with the small screw that is included with the mould. Lay the dowel (provided with the mould) across the top of the mould. Pull the wick fairly taut and wrap it round the dowel. To further ensure that the wick is sealed at the bottom of the mould, stick a small piece of florists' putty or mould sealer round the screw and wick hole. You can also use masking tape for this purpose. Use a 1½" to 2" high aluminum pan or pie dish as a safety pan under your mould—just in case the sealer doesn't hold.

Spray a small amount of mould release into the mould, taking care not to use too much. Test the temperature of the melted wax and, as soon as it registers 185° F. (85° C.), add stearic acid (3 tablespoons per pound of wax) and stir until it is dissolved. Then shave off enough dye from the dye chip to color

Illus. 1. These are the basic materials needed for candle-making: (from left to right) candle dye, an oven mitt, wax heating container, candle thermometer, mottling oil, mould release, stearic acid (on plate), candle mould, wick and dowel, and a bucket for use in cooling the candle.

the wax. Stir until the dye is dissolved. Add scent, if desired (1 teaspoon per pound of wax).

Fill the plastic or metal container with water. This serves as a water bath in which to cool the mould. Make sure there is enough water to come up to the level of the wax in the mould. Have a light weight on hand in case the filled mould starts to float.

When the melted wax has reached a temperature of 195° F. (91° C.) pour the wax (using an oven mitt) to within ½ inch of the top of the mould. Let the mould stand for about half a minute and then place it in the water bath (Illus. 2). Take care that no water runs into the mould and, if it starts to float, place a weight across the top of the mould.

Illus. 2. Place the filled mould in a bucket of cold water to cool.

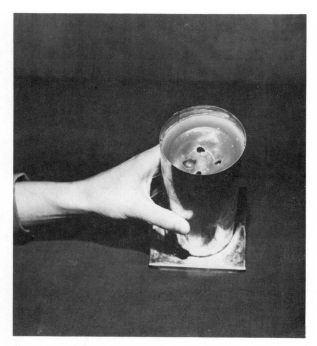

Illus. 3. Puncture a few holes in the wax crust to open the air pocket resulting from wax shrinkage.

The candle will begin to form as the wax hardens from the outside toward the center. Since wax shrinks as it cools, a depression will form around the wick. As soon as a thin film has formed across the top of the wax, remove the mould from the water bath and place it on a level table. After about an hour, take a wooden dowel or knitting needle and puncture the wax shell in three places about one inch from the wick. Be sure to poke the dowel or needle to within one inch of the bottom of the mould. This releases the entrapped air and results in a better-burning candle.

Heat the wax left from the original pour to the same temperature, 195° F. (91° C.), at which the candle was poured. Fill the entire cavity with wax, but be careful not to fill above the wax level of the original pour. If the mould is over-filled at this point, molten wax will run down the side of the candle in the mould, making it difficult to remove the candle and ruining the finish. For large candles, you may need to poke and refill the cavity two or three times.

Let the candle cool until both the mould and the wax are cool to the touch. Now, remove the wick sealing screw and wick sealer (if used) and pull the wick at the bottom of the mould straight. This end of the wick will be the end that burns.

Gently squeeze the sides of the mould. You can feel and hear the wax separate from the sides of the mould.

Illus. 4. Trim the seam line and any other imperfections with a sharp knife.

Turn the mould over and gently tap the bottom of the mould with your hand until the candle slides out. If the candle sticks in the mould, allow it to cool for a longer period and try again. If this does not work, place the mould in the refrigerator for half an hour.

If you still have trouble, scrape the small film of wax away from the top of the mould, all the way round the candle. Use your fingernail or a blunt object, but take care not to scratch the sides of the mould. As a last resort, run hot water over the sides and bottom of the mould until the candle slides free. This should be done only if all else fails, as it mars the finish of the candle.

Trim the seam line and the bottom of the candle with a knife (Illus. 4), cut the wick to a length of ½ inch, and your candle is finished and ready for burning.

The procedure for making the block candle is basically the same technique used to make all other candles in this book. Remember, *always* add stearic acid to the wax and *always* spray the mould with mould release, except where otherwise noted.

Layer Candles

There are many variations on the basic block candle. Try making a colorful layer candle first. They are fun to make, and you can apply the basic technique to other, more difficult candles. (Illus. 5 shows a few layer candles.)

Melt several cans of 145° F. (63° C.) melting point wax and add stearic acid to each can. Select a different dye for each can of wax and stir it in. Wick

the mould, seal the wick, and spray mould release into the mould, and, when the wax reaches a temperature of 195° F. (91° C.), pour the first layer. Place the mould into the water bath for a few minutes and then remove it. As soon as the wax has a firm, but warm, film across the top, heat the next can of wax and pour it in. Immerse the mould in water for a few minutes and then remove. Continue this procedure until you reach the desired height. After the candle has cooled for about an hour, puncture holes in the wax and, when it has cooled to the touch, fill the hole resulting from wax shrinkage. When the mould and wax are cool to the touch, remove the candle and finish it.

Sometimes the cooled layer pulls away from the side of the mould before the next layer is poured. When the finished candle is taken from the mould trim off the thin pieces of wax that have seeped down with a knife. Polish the candle with a damp paper towel or piece of nylon to remove any blemishes.

There are many possible variations of the layer candle. Try pouring alternating thick and thin layers. Or pour many colors of wax in very thin layers. Just remember to pour each layer before the previous one has completely cooled. Otherwise the layers will not adhere to each other.

TILTED LAYER CANDLES

You can make a completely different type of layer candle by simply tilting the mould for each layer.

Prepare your mould by wicking it and sealing the hole. Spray a small amount of mould release into the mould. Melt and dye enough wax for the various layers and find an object with which to tilt the mould.

Tilt the mould (Illus. 6) and pour the first layer. When the wax is ready for the second layer, tilt the

Illus. 5. There are many possibilities for layer candles. Try making thick and thin layers, or alternating colors, or making each layer a different color.

Illus. 6. Tilt the mould in a different direction for each successive layer.

mould in a different direction and pour. Continue this process until you are ready to pour the last layer.

Pour the last layer with the mould level so the base of the candle will be flat. Fill the hole caused by shrinkage and, when the mould is cool to the touch, remove the wick screw and sealer, remove the candle from the mould, and finish.

If any wax has run down between the sides of the mould and the candle, you can either trim it off and polish the sides of the candle or leave it on for the effect it produces.

Mottled Candles

A mottled candle is distinguished by small, snow-flake-like crystals in the wax (Illus. 7). These are formed by the addition of a small amount of mottling oil or mineral oil. Make them in much the same way as the block candle but omit the stearic acid, since it will inhibit the mottling.

Melt and dye a few pounds of 145° F. (63 °C.) melting point wax. String the wick through the wick hole, pull it taut, and wrap it round the dowel. Mottled candles do not require mould release or the water bath. The oil acts as a mould release and, because the candle must cool very slowly for the mottling to take place, the water bath is omitted.

As soon as the mould is ready for pouring, bring the wax up to 160° F. (71° C.) and mix in 3 table-spoons of oil for every pound of wax. If you want more mottling, add more oil; for less mottling add less oil and cool the candle faster. As soon as the oil has been stirred into the wax, pour the wax into the mould to the proper height. Now, place the mould on a level surface and put a paper bag or cardboard box over it to ensure that it cools slowly. When the mould is cool to the touch fill the cavity resulting from shrinkage. After the candle has completely cooled, remove the wick screw and mould sealer. Now slide the candle out of the mould and finish. There may be a small amount of oil on the outside of the candle. Just wipe this away with a tissue.

If the candle did not mottle, one of three things could have happened: either the wax was poured at

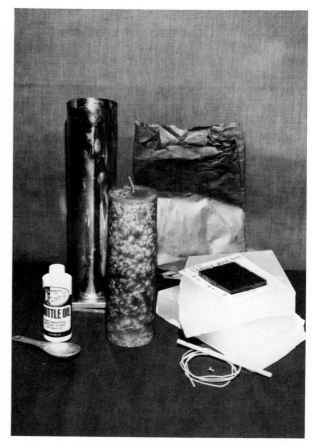

Illus. 7. Mottled candles require only wax, mottling oil, a mould and wick, and candle dye.

too high a temperature, it cooled too rapidly, or not enough oil was added. Also, certain dyes inhibit mottling. Green, for example, allows only very small mottles to form.

Mottling is very effective when used in layer candles. Interesting effects can also be obtained by alternating mottled and plain layers of wax.

2
Moulded Forms

There are many interesting ways in which to use the basic block candle mould. You can make candles with rough or smooth surfaces, candles with objects imbedded in them, hollow "hurricane" candles, glow-through candles, and many others, as well as variations and combinations of the different styles.

Chunk Candles

First make the chunks. Chunks are available in craft shops, but it's more fun, and cheaper, to make your own. Make them in the same way you would fudge. Take a fudge pan or cookie sheet and spray it with mould release. Pour in 145° F. (63° C.) melting point wax, heated to 195° F. (91° C.), to whatever thickness you wish your chunks to be. You should add extra stearic acid so the chunks will be harder than the regular candle wax and withstand the temperature of the hot wax being poured over them. Let the wax cool until it is fairly hard across the entire surface. Cut the wax into squares (Illus. 8). Let the wax cool completely and cut through the original cuts. Turn the pan over and pop the chunks out. Repeat this procedure with several different colors.

Now melt about a pound (depending on the size of your candle) of 135° F. (57° C.) melting point wax. Use either no dye at all, or a very light shade. If the wax is dark, the color of the chunks will not show through. Heat the wax to 180° F. (82° C.) and string the wick through the mould.

Half fill the mould with the melted wax and pour in the different chunks. Fill the mould to the top with chunks, and push them down firmly. Add more molten wax until it covers the chunks at the top of the mould. Put the mould in a water bath for a few minutes, then remove it and place on a level surface to cool. When the mould is cool to the touch, remove the wick sealer and slide the chunk candle out.

If you wish to make the chunks protrude, hold the candle by the wick (after the candle has been removed from the mould) and place it in water heated to 180° F. (88° C.). Because the chunks are made from a harder wax than the surrounding wax, the clear wax will melt away and the chunks will remain. The longer you leave the candle in the water, the more the chunks will protrude. You can also remove some of the wax with a knife after it has been warmed by the water.

Illus. 8. Cut the wax into squares before it has completely cooled.

You can give your candle a nice finish just by dipping it into cold water. After you take it out of the hot water, touch the bottom to a smooth, level surface, such as a clean tabletop, to level off any drops of wax. Then immerse the candle in cold water for about a minute. Let the candle cool completely, and then polish it with a piece of nylon.

Flower Fantasy Candle

The flower fantasy candle is fun to make and offers many possibilities for design. Take a 2-inch-diameter mould and string and seal the wick. Heat clear wax to a temperature of 195° F. (91° C.), and add stearic acid. Use 145° F. (63° C.) melting point wax (use this wax for all candles, except where otherwise noted). Pour the cylinder mould full and place it in a water bath for a few minutes. Then remove the mould and place it on a level surface to cool.

Select several small- or medium-size plastic flowers or plants, or both, and cut them from their stems. (Other objects, such as aluminum foil, can be substituted or added.) Remove the 2-inch-diameter candle from the mould (after it has hardened) and trim the wax away from the wick until it looks like a sharpened pencil. Attach the flowers and leaves to this core candle in attractive positions. Now, gently slide the candle into a 3-inch diameter mould and insert the wick through the wick hole. Seal the wick hole and place the mould upright.

Position the core candle in the center of the mould and slowly pour clear wax into the mould. Place the mould in a water bath for a few minutes, then remove and allow it to cool. If a wax shrinkage cavity appears, fill it with hot wax. When the wax is cool, slide the candle out. For a more glossy appearance on the candle, rub the surface with a damp paper towel or piece of nylon.

You can make the flowers stand out in relief, if you wish. Just immerse the candle in water heated to 200° F. (93° C.) until the desired amount of wax has been removed.

Crushed Ice Candles

Crushed ice candles are made in much the same fashion as the flower fantasy candle. Make the core candle (use a dye, if you wish, for this candle), insert it in the larger mould, and string and seal the wick. Place the mould on a level surface and fill the surrounding sides with crushed ice. Now pour wax heated to 195° F. (91° C.) over the crushed ice until the mould is full. Allow the wax to cool and slide the candle out of the mould.

When the candle is removed, the water will run from the pockets formed by the ice. By using the inner core, water is prevented from accumulating round the wick and good burning is assured.

Hurricane Candles

Hurricane candles are attractive and can last indefinitely. They are really wax shells with votive candles in the middle. The votive candles give off enough light to glow through the wax shell of the hurricane candle and can be replaced when they burn out.

Use a mould that has a diameter of at least 4 inches. Seal the wick hole, but do not put in a wick. Melt enough wax to fill the mould and add stearic acid and dye, if desired. To insure a stronger shell, you can also add 1 teaspoon of plastic additive per pound of wax (see page 38). Now bring the temperature of the

wax up to 190° F. (88° C.) and fill the mould to within ½ inch of the top. Place the mould in the water bath until the wax hardens around the outside edge to a thickness of ¼ inch (Illus. 9). Remove the mould and pour the excess wax back into its original container (Illus. 10 and 11). Set the mould on a level surface to cool.

Once the inside of the hurricane candle is cool, remove it from the mould (Illus. 12). Trim the top edge until it is even and set the candle aside for the moment.

Votive candles are available in most stores, but you can make them with no trouble at all. Dye and scent the

Illus. 9. Let the wax harden for a few minutes.

Illus. 10. Pour the wax back into the container.

Illus. 11. The wax shell in the mould should be about ¼ inch thick.

Illus. 12. Remove the wax shell from the mould and then place a votive candle inside.

wax, and heat it to 180° F. (82° C.). Place a small paper cup or glass on a level surface and pour about 3 inches of wax into it. Let it cool and, if you used a paper cup, peel the paper off. If you used a glass, you can either slide the candle out of the glass or leave it in. If the candle is difficult to remove, place it in the refrigerator for a few minutes or run hot water over it.

To insert the wick, either drill a small hole through the candle or take a metal knitting needle or coat hanger, heat it up over a burner, and melt a hole through the candle. Insert the wick into the hole. If the hole is too large, pour a small amount of molten wax into it and then quickly insert the wick. Votive candles can also be wicked with a Wick Holder Tab and a metal core wick.

Now, place the votive candle in the center of the shell, and your hurricane candle is finished. Whenever the votive candle burns out just replace it with another.

VARIATIONS ON THE HURRICANE CANDLE

There are several ways to make the basic hurricane candle more interesting. First, try making a hurricane candle with a cut-out design.

Make a regular hurricane shell, following the directions on page 6. After you have poured the wax out, take a knife, reach into the mould, and cut out a design in the wax. Remove the pieces that you cut out as you go along. Now pour the mould full of a different color wax and place it back into the water. Allow the wax to form another wax shell about ¼ inch thick and pour the remaining wax back into its original container. When the wax shell has cooled, remove it from the mould and trim the top. Place a votive candle in the middle of the shell. (See Illus. 12.)

You can also create swirling, abstract designs on the hurricane shell. Take two small cans and melt a few ounces of colored wax (two different colors) in each one. Heat the wax to between 160°–170° F. (71°–77° C.). Spray the mould with mould release. Don't worry about spraying too much in the mould. If you do, it adds a bit of texture to the surface of the finished candle.

Pour a small amount of one color into the bottom of the mould. Now, hold the mould in your hands and tilt and turn it so that the small rivulets of wax make an interesting design. If the mould gets too warm, submerge it in the water bath for a few seconds. After you have finished with the first color, pour it back into the container. Pour in the next color and repeat the process.

Heat a large container of wax to 170° F. (77° C.). You can color this or just add stearic acid to make it white. Pour a small amount of the wax into the bottom of the mould. Slowly pour the wax back into the container, turning the mould as you do so that the wax coats the entire surface of the mould.

Do this several times, or until you have built up a thin shell over the abstract designs. If the mould becomes too warm and the designs begin to melt, hold the mould in the water bath for a few seconds. Let the wax shell cool for a minute or so. Now pour the mould full just as you did for the regular hurricane candle. Place it in the water bath until a shell has formed that is ¼ inch thick. Remove the mould from the water and pour the remaining wax back into its container. Let the shell cool, then remove it from the mould and trim the top. Place a votive candle in the middle. Your candle is ready to burn. (See Illus. 13.)

Abstract and Cut-Out Design Block Candles

The abstract and cut-out design techniques which were explained earlier can also be applied to regular

Illus. 13. With good care, your beautiful hurricane candle can last forever.

block candles (Illus. 14). The procedure is exactly the same, with one exception—a wick is used when making the shell.

Make the shell, using either an abstract or cut-out design. Now fill the mould with wax heated to 170° F. (77° C.) and place it in the water bath. Let the entire amount of wax cool this time. When a thin film of wax forms on the top, remove the mould from the water bath. After an hour, puncture some small

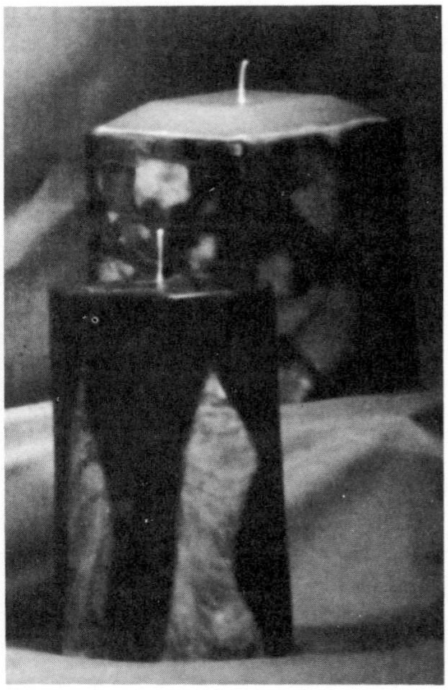

Illus. 14. These abstract and cut-out design block candles are merely hurricane candles filled with wax.

holes in the crust around the wick. When the wax has cooled and shrunk, pour the hollow full with wax heated to 190° F. (88° C.). Once this has cooled, remove the candle from the mould.

Remember that these candles often look good with a textured surface, so don't be afraid to use a larger amount of mould release.

Glow-Through Candles

Glow-through candles are basically just block candles dipped in wax. Like the abstract and cut-out design block candles, they have an interesting and beautiful appearance that is improved, rather than destroyed, by burning.

Make a regular block candle, in any type of mould, using clear wax. After the candle has cooled, remove it from the mould. Hold the candle by the wick and dip it into colored wax heated to about 190° F. (88° C.). Make the first dip the longest. Swirl the candle round to melt off any scale and rough edges. Let the candle cool a minute and dip again with a smooth in-and-out movement. Do not leave the candle in the hot wax longer than a few seconds. Repeat this process until the color coating has been formed on the outside of the candle.

Try making a multi-colored glow-through candle. Dip the entire candle into yellow four times. Be sure that the first dip is longer than the others. Now dip two-thirds of the candle into red three times. Then dip one-third of the candle into blue three times. The pink dipped over the yellow turns orange and the blue dipped over the red turns purple. These candles, when burned, give off a beautiful, warm, glowing light.

3

Sand-Cast Candles

Sand-cast candles are the most varied of all candles. They can be made in almost any shape—square, round, triangular, or free-form—and size, and with or without sand. You can use sand of any color and texture—from fine grains to small pebbles—depending on the effect you want to create. (Sand can be collected from beaches, streams, or quarries, or purchased from lumberyards and garden supply shops.)

You can use almost any large container to hold the sand. Plastic dishpans, wood boxes, sheet metal boxes, and cardboard boxes lined with plastic wrap are all suitable. Choose a container that will not rust or decompose through contact with the moist sand.

Always dampen the sand prior to making the form. Add enough water to turn the sand a dark color. Test the firmness by taking a small handful and squeezing it. If it holds its shape in your open hand without falling apart, it is the right consistency. If the sand has too much water it will be muddy and stick to your hand. If this happens, just add more dry sand until the right consistency is reached.

Make the impression in the sand in one of two ways: either dig a hole in the sand with your hands or press a form—a can, a block of wood, a bowl, or any suitable object—into the sand and pack the sand round it. Either method can produce a variety of results.

Sand Candles

A good sand candle must have a thick crust of sand round it after it has been removed from the sand. There are three important factors involved in getting this thick crust: the pouring temperature of the wax; the dampness of the sand; and the compactness of the sand. You must heat the wax to a temperature between 275°–300° F. (135°–149° C.). *(Observe every safety precaution when working with wax at these temperatures—serious burns can result from improper or casual handling of the wax.)* Use at least a 145° F. (63° C.) melting point wax. Anything less could combust at these high temperatures. Stand close by the burner, and check the temperature of the wax constantly to make sure that it does not exceed 300° F. (149° C.). The 145° F. (63° C.) wax will not combust until it reaches temperatures well above 400° F. (204° C.) but that

doesn't mean that you shouldn't be careful! When heating wax to these temperatures, make sure you use a container that is seamless so there will be no danger of leaks. Seamless coffee pots are sold in all hardware shops, and are also available in many second-hand shops.

The compactness and dampness of the sand are also of great importance. Be sure that you pack the sand firmly and evenly and, as mentioned earlier, be sure that it is just the right consistency. Otherwise the finished candle will be imperfect.

Dig a hole in the sand that is large enough to fit the form. Use a glass jar, a bowl, a piece of wood, or anything that comes to mind. Place the form into the hole and force it firmly into the sand. Pack the sand at least 3 inches from all sides of the form (Illus. 15). Remove the form slowly so that the sand remains intact.

If you want legs on the candle, take a wooden dowel or pencil and wrap tape round it about ½ inch from the end. Now push the dowel into the sand in

Illus. 15. Pack the sand round whatever form you use.

Illus. 16. The legs of your sand candle will all be uniform if you use some tape to mark the depth.

Illus. 17. Pour the hot wax directly onto the spoon. Otherwise the wax will erode a hole in the sand.

three places (or more, if you wish), using the tape to mark the depth of the holes (Illus. 16).

Place a small amount of wax in the bottom of the pot and melt it over a low flame. You only need to melt an inch or two of wax. Now add the rest of the wax, and turn the flame up higher. Remember to check the temperature of the wax frequently. Because it is being heated over a direct flame, the wax will heat up fairly quickly. If the wax starts to smoke and crack and pop, don't be alarmed. The smoking is normal and the other noises are due to small amounts of water in the wax. This won't hurt anything and is not dangerous. In fact, if large amounts of water are present in the wax, the wax will bubble and crack until all the water has evaporated. Heat the wax to at least 275° F. (135° C.).

Do not add dye to the wax. At these high temperatures it may become dark and muddy. Dyed wax is added later. With your oven mitt, take the seamless container and a spoon and get ready to pour. Hold the spoon in the middle of the hole near the bottom and pour the hot wax over it into the hole (Illus. 17). By pouring the wax over the spoon, you prevent the wax from eroding the sand at the bottom of the hole. Pour slowly and carefully so the wax does not splatter onto your hand. Fill the hole up to the top and place the container of wax in a safe place—*not* back on the burner!

You will notice that the wax bubbles and hisses. This is caused by contact with the damp sand. When this stops, the level of the wax will have dropped about 1 inch because that amount seeps into the sand.

Let the wax cool until it has a thick film across the surface. Take an ice pick, coat hanger, or nail and poke a wick hole into the middle of the candle. Try *not* to force it all the way through and out the bottom. Place the wick (use a wire core wick) into this hole. Make sure it is long enough to extend well above the surface of the sand.

When the wax is fairly hard (you need not wait until it is completely cold), dig down beneath the candle and lift it out of the sand. Lightly brush away some of the sand and set it down to dry. The sand is dry when its color changes from dark to light. This may take 7 or 8 hours.

You now have a sand shell that extends up from the candle on all sides. Brush any loose sand away, but take care not to break away the sides of the shell. With a knife, trim the top of the shell to make it even, and level the bottom. Set the candle on a level surface and pull the wick straight.

Now, heat some wax to a temperature of 210° F. (99° C.), this time in the double boiler, and add a little plastic additive (see page 38). Once the plastic has melted, add dye and let the wax cool to 170° F.

Illus. 18. Fill the wax shell to the top with dyed wax.

Illus. 19. You can use a torch to seal all the sand to the wax.

You can also use plastic spray finish to finish your sand candle, either in combination with torching or instead of torching.

SAND CANDLE VARIATIONS

There are many ways to vary your sand candles. (Illus. 20 shows some examples.) You can place sea shells, rocks, driftwood, plastic flowers, or any interesting object on the edge of the candle. If the object is small, add it just before you pour the last layer of wax. If it is large, place it in the sand before you pour any wax (Illus. 21).

Try making a cluster of sand candles. Form two or more holes, all within 1 inch of each other, and pour wax heated to at least 275° F. (135° C.) into each hole. The wax soaks through the inch of sand and binds the separate candles into one unit. Trim and

Illus. 20. You can make sand-cast candles in almost any shape you wish.

(77° C.). Pour the wax to the top of the shell and let it cool (Illus. 18). If any shrinkage appears, pour in a little more hot wax. You now have a fine sand candle.

You can give your sand candle an attractive finish with a propane torch. Make sure all the sand has dried, and brush off any excess. Place the candle in a container of some sort to catch any drips. Begin at the top of the candle, running the flame over the sand and wax with smooth, quick, brushing motions. Keep the flame very low. Once the top has a good finish, run the flame over the sides of the candle (Illus. 19). You'll see the sand begin to change color, from light to dark. Don't leave the flame in any one spot for too long or the sand will melt off. Continue to brush the sand with the flame until all the sand has changed color. A propane torch can be used to finish any type of candle.

Illus. 21. Driftwood is an attractive addition to sand candles.

pour the final layer just as you did for the single sand candle.

Cutting out pieces from the side of the sand crust makes a unique and beautiful candle. The technique is relatively simple. All you need, in addition to the materials already mentioned, is a baster.

Make a shape in the sand and fill it with wax heated to at least 275° F. (135° C.). Let the wax set in the sand until it begins to cloud at the bottom. Now take the baster and remove all the wax from the sand (Illus. 22). Just squirt it back into the original container. When the sand shell is empty, fill it with cold water and let it stand for about 20 minutes.

Remove the water with the baster and then remove

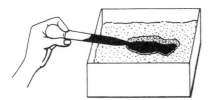

Illus. 22. Remove the liquid wax with an ordinary baster.

the empty sand shell from the sand. Handle the shell carefully. Take a sharp pointed knife and begin twisting a hole through the shell. Gently enlarge the hole until you feel it has a pleasing shape (Illus. 23). Pick another spot and do the same thing. Continue the process round the candle and then trim and smooth all the holes.

Place the sand shell back into the sand. Hold one hand inside the shell and with the other, pack sand up around the outside. The sand should not be too dry or too damp. Try to keep the sand out of the shell. As you pack it make sure that, where there are holes in the shell, the sand is flush with the inside of the shell. Do this all the way round the candle.

Heat some dyed wax to 170° F. (77° C.) and pour it into the shell to within ½ inch of the top. Let this wax cool and, when it forms a thin crust, place a wick in the middle. When the wax has cooled completely,

Illus. 23. Be very careful that you don't break the shell as you make the holes.

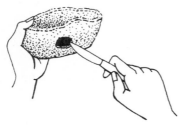

remove the candle from the sand, and brush. Let the sand dry.

Because the wax is poured at a low temperature, very little sand will stick to it where holes have been made in the shell. The little that does can easily be scraped off.

After it has dried, trim the top of the shell with a knife until it is even and smooth. Place the candle on a level surface and fill the last ½ inch with wax of a different color. Pour the wax at 170° F. (77° C.). When this layer cools, brush any excess sand off and finish, if you wish.

When little or no sand is desired, all you need do is heat the wax to a lower temperature. A layer candle, set off by a piece of driftwood, looks especially good when all the sand is scraped off (Illus. 24).

Dig a hole in the sand and gently pack the sand around the sides. If you want to place a piece of driftwood into the hole, clean it and brush off all the sand. Level the bottom of the hole with a flat object.

Layer separation is a common occurrence with these candles. To prevent this, add a little microcrystalline wax (sometimes sold by the name of shaping or sculpting wax) to each can of wax (1 part microcrystalline wax to 20 parts regular wax). This helps cement the layers to each other.

Pour the first layer to the desired thickness with wax heated to 190° F. (88° C.). Let this layer cool until about 1 inch of the wax is hard all round the edges. Now pour the second layer. When about 1 inch of wax is hard round the edges of this layer, poke a hole in the middle for the wick. Try not to go through the bottom of the candle. Insert enough wick to extend beyond the top of the sand.

Illus. 24. Watching this unusual candle burning is truly a delight.

Pour the remaining layers at the same temperature as the first two layers, following the same procedure. When you are ready to pour the last layer, let the previous layer cool until the hole caused by shrinkage appears. Then pour the last layer at a temperature of 210° F. (99° C.) to make sure it adheres.

When you can press the top layer without making an indentation, remove the candle from the sand. Dig under the candle and lift it out of the hole. Brush off the loose sand and, with the edge of a knife, scrape the sand from the wax until the different layers appear. Remove all the sand this way and polish the candle with a nylon stocking or damp paper towel.

There is an easier alternative to scraping the sand off with a knife. You can use a propane torch to help remove the sand and, at the same time, give your candle a nice finish.

Brush as much sand off the candle as possible and place it in a container. Heat up the wax round the top edge of the candle with a low flame from the torch. After this area has been heated a little, scrape off the sand with the edge of a knife. Don't dig into the wax any deeper than is required to remove the sand. Keep working round the candle in this manner until all the sand has been removed. There will always be a small amount of sand left on the candle, but don't spend too much time trying to remove it.

Clean the top and sides of the candle with a small brush. Now go over the top of the candle with a low flame from the torch. You can use it like a paint-brush. After the top has a nice finish, begin working along the sides and edges. You can make interesting curves and grooves along the sides of the candle or, if you want to preserve the original shape of the candle, you can just run the flame quickly over the wax.

If your candle includes a piece of driftwood, or some other object, and you want to give it a nice, glossy finish, just melt a few pieces of wax on it.

After you get the feel of the torch, and have a good understanding of its possibilities, try experimenting. You can use it to create all sorts of unique patterns and designs.

Aluminum Foil Candles

You can use aluminum foil to make solid or layered candles. Just form a shape in the sand, place a single piece of foil into it, and mould the foil to the shape. If you wish, you can add objects to the edge of the candle, in the same way you did for the sand candle.

Heat the wax to about 195° F. (91° C.). If you make a layered candle, follow the directions given for a layered sand candle (page 12). If you make a solid candle, just pour the wax, put in the wick, fill up the shrinkage, and so on (Illus. 25). After the candle has cooled, peel off the foil (Illus. 26). It's as simple as that. The result is a glossy, fine-looking candle with no trace of sand on it.

Illus. 25. Pour the wax into a single sheet of aluminum foil.

Illus. 26. Aluminum foil candles have a unique texture and appearance, and you can form them into whatever shape pleases your fancy.

4

Hand-Formed and Taper Candles

Hand-formed and taper candles are quite easy to make and offer wide possibilities for design. Furthermore, an understanding of the techniques used to make these candles is essential in constructing appliqué and painted candles. So try making a few—they're fun to make, attractive, and a stepping-stone to more intricate and complicated candles.

Hand-Formed Candles

The first step, when forming a shape from wax, is to soften the wax. Microcrystalline or sculpting wax may be added to keep the wax more pliable. There are two ways to soften the wax, both of which produce the same result.

The first method involves heating the wax in the oven. Melt a large piece of 135° F. (57° C.) melting point wax, pour it into a cake pan, or something similar, and let it cool until it is hard enough to be removed. Make the layer fairly thin; otherwise it will take a great deal of time to soften. After you have removed the wax from the pan, wrap it in an old towel. Turn on your oven, leaving it at the lowest temperature, and place the wrapped wax on a rack. The towel prevents any melted wax from dripping and can easily be washed out in hot water afterwards.

Test the wax every few minutes. When it can be twisted and formed without breaking, remove it from the oven and form it into whatever shape you wish.

If you have a heat lamp it is a good idea to work under it. Otherwise, if the wax becomes too hard to work with, just place it back in the oven for a few minutes. After you get the shape you want, poke a hole through the middle with an ice pick or coat hanger. Insert the wick and press the wax around the top of it. Place the wax form in cold water and just let it float until it is hard.

After your form has cooled, remove it from the water, dry with a towel and set it aside until it is completely dry. Then hold the form by the wick and dip it into dyed wax heated to 190° F. (88° C.) several times. This gives the form a coat of color and covers all creases, cracks and imperfections.

The second method is also simple, and produces the same results. Heat some 135° F. (57° C.) melting point wax to a temperature of 150° F. (66° C.). Fill

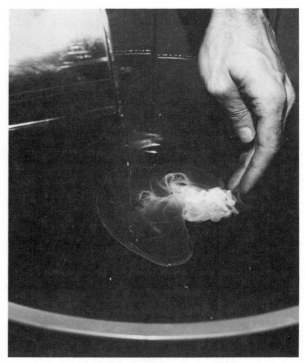

Illus. 27. As you pour the hot wax into the water, splash a little water onto it to cool it. You can then handle it without burning your hands.

a large pail with cold water. Now pour the melted wax slowly into the water (Illus. 27). Splash cold water over the top of the molten wax to cool it. The wax is still molten in the middle, but it is not warm enough to burn your hands. Take the edges of the wax and bend them towards the middle (Illus. 28). Slowly submerge the entire mass and begin squeezing (Illus. 29). Make sure all the wax is under the water or the liquid wax will squirt into the air. Knead the wax until it is firm but still soft. Remove the mass of wax from the water, flatten it, and place it on a towel. Fold the towel over the wax and press, rub, and dry (Illus. 30). Form the soft wax into whatever shape you wish. Insert the wick just as you did in the earlier example. This method may seem complicated, but it is quite easy and not half as messy as it sounds.

Place the finished form in cold water and follow the procedures for drying and dipping as you did before.

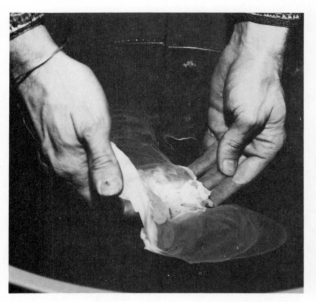

Illus. 28. Fold the edges of the pool of wax towards the middle.

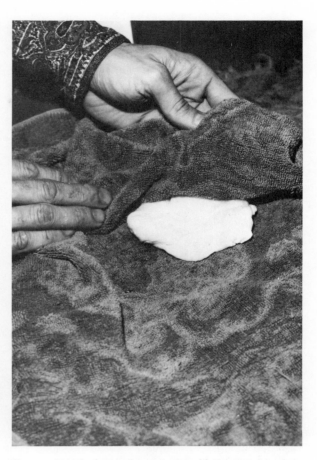

Illus. 30. Dry the lump of wax in a towel. Don't worry about wax ruining the towel—the wax will come right out when washed.

Illus. 29. Slowly put the mass of wax under the water and squeeze.

Taper Candles

You can make tapers with moulds or by hand dipping—either fat and short or long and thin. Use either 135° F. (57° C.) or 145° F. (63° C.) melting point wax to make tapers. However, for the long, thin Danish tapers, special wax is available that has a high plastic content.

Dipping tapers is a slow process, but rewarding. The container size used for the dip tank depends on how many tapers you wish to dip at once. Begin with two, using one long wick doubled over to form two wicks. A weight such as a washer, nut, or paper clip can be tied to the end of the wick to help insure making a straight dipped taper. Use clear wax for the bulk of the candle, and colored wax for the last four or five dips.

The secret of dipping lies in the temperature of the wax. Keep the temperature within 10° to 20° F. (5° to 11° C.) of the melting point of the wax. Each time you dip the wick into the wax, you want the maximum amount of wax to build up around it. If the wax is too cool, a film will form on the surface and the taper will have bubbles and imperfections. If the wax is too hot, no wax will build up on the wick. So, it is best to keep the temperature of the wax fairly low.

Dip the wick into the wax for a second and withdraw it. Then immerse the wick in a bucket of water for a few seconds and dry it with a small towel. Make sure that no droplets of water remain on the wax. Repeat this process until you have reached a satisfactory thickness (Illus. 31). Trim the bottom of the taper with a knife to make it even, or shorter, and your candle is ready for burning.

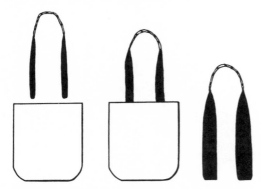

Illus. 31. You can make your tapers any size you wish when you dip them by hand.

If you want to give the tapers as gifts or use them for decoration, string a few beads onto the middle of the wick before you double it over. These look very attractive when the two tapers hang from the common wick.

CUT-OUT TAPERS

Making cut-out tapers is fairly easy. Dip your taper in one color of wax until it is about $\frac{1}{2}$ inch in diameter (thicker for larger candles). Then dip it into another color until you have built up the wax another $\frac{1}{2}$ inch. Dip the taper in a few more colors and cool it a few seconds in cold water. Now cut designs into the tapers with a knife until all the different colors show through (Illus. 32).

Illus. 32. Don't make the cuts in your candle too deep—if you do, the candle will droop over when the flame reaches the cut-out.

DANISH TAPERS

Danish tapers are made in the same fashion. If you do not find Danish taper wax available, you can make up a close duplicate by adding one part stearic acid and one part plastic additive to every twenty parts of wax. Make the Danish taper in the same way you made the regular taper. After the color coat has been added, curve the taper slightly before placing it into the water to cool. The addition of the stearic acid and plastic additive keeps the taper from drooping in warm weather. It also increases the burning time.

You can make interesting taper trees from Danish tapers. Dip four or more tapers and place them on a

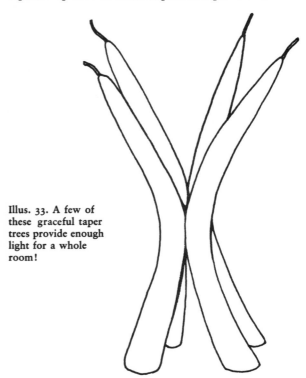

Illus. 33. A few of these graceful taper trees provide enough light for a whole room!

clean surface. Take two tapers at a time and firmly squeeze them together just a little distance from the bottom until they stick. Dip the bottoms in hot wax a few times so they are held together firmly, then hold the two tapers at the bottom and dip them into cold water. The cold water will cause the wax to set so the tapers will not droop. Take the other two tapers and press them together just as you did the first two tapers. After you have dipped the bottoms in hot wax and set the shape with cold water, hold the two sets together and dip them into hot wax until they are firmly attached to each other. (See Illus. 33.)

BEESWAX TAPERS

Beeswax is available in colored sheets at most craft shops. To make beeswax tapers, strip the paper from the sheet of beeswax, place the wick along one edge (Illus. 34) and roll the sheet round the wick (Illus. 35).

Illus. 34. Beeswax tapers are, obviously, just about the simplest candles to make.

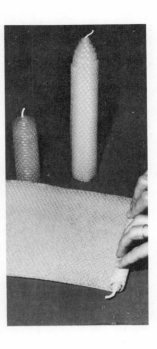

Illus. 35. After you have rolled the sheet of beeswax into a candle, you might want to try squeezing and moulding it into an interesting shape.

5

Appliqué Candles

Appliqué techniques hold almost endless possibilities for the candle-maker. Many techniques are detailed in the following pages, but don't restrict yourself to these—they are merely the foundation for more designs. Use your imagination and don't be afraid to try something new or unconventional. If you have any trouble making these candles, just practice a bit. Very few beautiful things are made on the first try.

Wax Appliqués

AN OWL CANDLE

Wax appliqué candles are really no more than candles decorated with pieces of wax. By hand-forming the pieces, you can create a wide range of original, hand-crafted candles.

For your first project, try making an owl. It's simple to make, and a good introduction to the techniques of appliqué. To make the owl you need some 135° F. (57° C.) melting point wax and a small can of microcrystalline wax. You can just substitute more 135° F. (57° C.) melting point wax if microcrystalline wax is not available.

Form a rough approximation of an owl with your hands (see the section on hand-forming starting on page 14). You do not need to be too accurate or detailed—the entire owl form will be covered with pieces of wax, and appliqué pieces provide the detail. Now melt three cans (or more) of the 135° F. (57° C.) melting point wax and add a different dye to each. Cut a length of wick and start dipping it in the first color. (The taper need only be about 9 or 10 inches long.) Instead of dipping the taper into water after every dip, as you did for the taper candle, just dip it into water after every three dips. After the ninth dip, leave the taper in the water for 20 seconds. Otherwise the wax might slip off the wick. Continue dipping until the taper is ½ inch thick. Now dip the taper in another color, following the same procedure, until you have another ring of color about the same size as the first.

Repeat this procedure for a third color. If you find the wax slipping off the wick, hold it in the water for a few seconds. You can use as many colors as you wish. For the final dipping, pick another color or re-peat the first color. After the final dip leave the taper in the water for about half a minute. Make sure that the wax is firm enough to handle, but still soft enough to work with.

Hold the wick in one hand and the top of the wax in the other. Gently pull the wick from the candle, holding the wax between your thumb and forefinger close to the wick (Illus. 36). Pull the wax entirely off the wick and wrap the wax form in a towel to keep it warm. The towel may then be placed in an oven at a very low temperature. This keeps the form soft and workable.

Dip the owl form into wax heated to 195° F. (91° C.) and hold it there for a minute. Remove it for a few

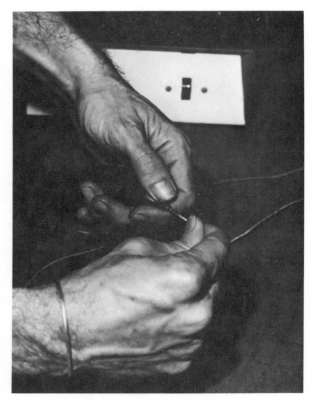

Illus. 36. Pull the wick out before the taper hardens.

Illus. 37. Slice the taper with a sharp knife.

Illus. 38. Don't press too hard when you attach the pieces of the eye together.

seconds and immerse it again—in and out quickly. Place the owl on a level surface under a heat lamp, if you have one. If you don't have one available, try to work in the warmest room or area in your house. Remove the taper from the towel and begin slicing it like you would a carrot (Illus. 37). Slice 5 or 6 pieces and stick them on the owl, beginning at the very bottom of the form. Use just enough pressure to hold the slices to the candle. Work around in circles and overlap each slice. Don't slice too many pieces at one time—they cool fast and will not stick onto the ball. Keep slicing and sticking the pieces on in an overlapping circular pattern until you reach the wick. Punch a hole in the last piece, slip it over the wick, and press it down onto the other pieces.

If you find the going slow and that the wax is getting too hard, melt a small can of 135° F. (57° C.) melting point wax or microcrystalline wax (microcrystalline wax is preferable because it is stickier) and place it next to you. Do not let the wax harden. Take a small paintbrush and, before you place a slice on the candle, brush a small amount of liquid wax cn the slice and a small amount on the candle, on the spot where the slice will go.

To make the eyes, slice six pieces for each eye. To make one eye lay six pieces in a circle with each piece overlapping and touching at a common center. Press the pieces together with your thumb and forefinger (Illus. 38). When they are firmly attached to one another, curl the ends up. Now roll a small piece of wax into a ball and place it in the middle of one eye. If the wax is not warm enough to stick, brush a little hot wax onto it (Illus. 39 and 40).

Illus. 39. Hot wax holds the ball of wax in place.

Illus. 40. These eyes, which are remarkably easy to make, add charm and personality to your owl.

Illus. 41. Brush plenty of hot wax on the back of the eye to ensure adhesion.

Brush some hot wax on the back of the eye and on the appropriate spot on the candle (Illus. 41). Hold the eye in place for a few seconds until it is securely attached (Illus. 42). Do the same for the other eye.

Cut a wedge-like slice from the taper and pull it into a long beak shape to make a nose (Illus. 43). Press it down onto the body of the owl until it sticks firmly (Illus. 44 and 45). If it is too cold, use some hot wax on a brush.

Although it is not absolutely necessary, a glaze finish protects your appliqué candle and makes it glossier. The glaze itself is nothing more than clear, molten wax, and is very simple to apply. (Plastic sprays are also available in craft shops, and are suitable glazes for candles.)

Different waxes give different finishes. For a high-gloss finish, use 155° F. (68° C.) melting point wax. 145° F. (63° C.) melting point wax gives a mat finish. You can tone down either of these waxes by adding a little 135° F. (57° C.) melting point wax. Experiment with other waxes—by blending different melting point waxes together, you can create your own unique finish.

To glaze your candle, heat a large quantity of the wax of your choice to a temperature of between 185°–200° F. (85°–93° C.)—185° F. (85° C.) for dark colored candles; higher temperatures for lighter candles. Make sure you melt enough to totally cover your candle. Also, fill a container with enough cold water to cover the candle.

Hold the candle by the wick (use pliers to avoid burning your fingers) and, in one smooth motion, dip the candle vertically into the melted wax. If the candle starts to float, push it straight down. As soon as the candle is completely immersed in the wax,

Illus. 42. Press the eye onto the owl form.

Illus. 43. A wedge shape makes an excellent nose.

Illus. 44. Attach the nose to the owl.

Illus. 45. Your owl is finished and ready for display.

Illus. 46 (left). Embellish your block candles with a few well-placed flowers.

pull it out in one smooth motion. Never apply more than one coat of glaze, or the color of the candle will be obscured.

Now, set the candle down for a second on a smooth, clean, level surface. You need to do no more than just touch it on the surface. Finally, dip the candle in the cold water for several seconds.

Often, when using a 155° F. (68° C.) melting point wax, small, hair-line cracks appear on the finish. To avoid this, just blend one part 135° F. (57° C.) melting point wax with three parts 155° F. (68° C.) melting point wax. This wax will flow into all the small nooks and crannies of the appliqué candle, and no cracks will appear.

FLOWERS

You can make simple flowers by the same method that you used to make the eyes on the owl. Choose any type of candle and attach these flowers to it. Make stems by stretching small pieces of green wax and attaching them underneath the flowers. Remember to use hot wax and a brush if the flowers and stems will not stick. Finish the candle after you attach the flowers and stems. (See Illus. 46.)

You can use tapers to form another type of simple, tasteful flower. Make a ball candle and dip it in wax heated to 195° F. (91° C.). Add dye to the wax if you wish. Slice a circle from a warm taper (made in the same way as the taper used in the owl candle) and place it on the ball. Slice off six more pieces, this time at an angle so the pieces will be elongated. Place them round the circle (Illus. 47). Now cut a small piece from the taper and stretch it into the shape of a stem (Illus. 48). Attach this to the candle under the flower (Illus. 49). Make another flower on the other side of the candle, and finish.

Illus. 47. Use slices from a warm taper to make these flowers.

Illus. 48. Use a piece of the taper to make a stem.

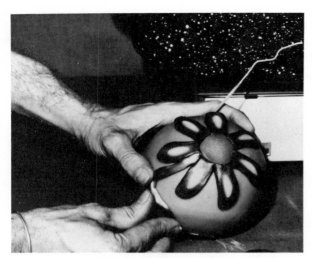

Illus. 49. Attach the stem to the lower part of the candle, underneath the flower.

OVERLAY BALL CANDLE

Overlay ball candles (Illus. 50) are fun to make and really no more than a variation on the owl candle. Make a ball candle and a multi-colored taper, and just follow the procedure detailed earlier for the owl candle. (Do not make the eyes though.)

Illus. 50. If you have some taper slices left over from the owl candle, try making an overlay ball candle.

TAPER FLOWERS

The next type of appliqué flower requires a bit of practice. First you need a small cylinder candle mould. Remove the wick from a warm taper (made according to the instructions on page 15). Place the taper in a towel while you dip the cylinder form into hot wax a few times to give it a coating of soft, sticky wax.

Remove the taper from the towel, cut the end off, and curl your thumb and forefinger round it about an inch from the end (Illus. 51). Squeeze and pull until you have a large piece of wax followed by a long thin piece about the width of a pencil (Illus. 52). When this piece is about 6 inches long, cut it from the rest of the taper.

You now have a long stem with a 1-inch diameter cylinder of wax on one end. Push your thumb about ½ inch into the end of the cylinder (Illus. 53). Press the

wax together between your thumb in the middle and your index and middle fingers on the outside. As you press, stretch a small amount of wax and curl it upwards (Illus. 54). Move your thumb and fingers over ½ inch and repeat (Illus. 55). Do this all round

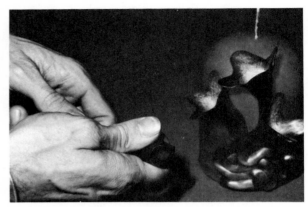

Illus. 51. Hold the end of the taper firmly as you begin to squeeze.

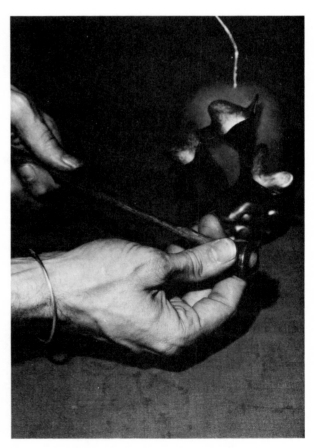

Illus. 52. Stretch the taper out into a long, thin shape, but leave the first inch thick.

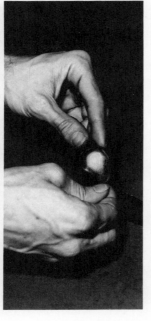

Illus. 53. Press your thumb into the thick end of the taper.

Illus. 54. Pull one edge of the wax cylinder upwards.

flatten it out (Illus. 57). Keep making flowers and attaching them until you feel the candle is finished. Again, you may need to warm the wax occasionally.

Glaze the candle with hot, melted wax.

You may come up with your own ideas for appliqués of this type. Try them out! By cutting, stretching, rolling, and shaping, you can make dozens of different flowers, leaves, stems and vines.

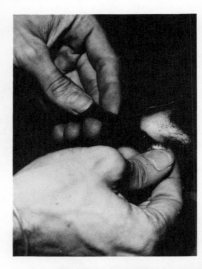

Illus. 56. Pull two or three more edges upwards. Try not to pull the rest of the taper out of shape as you do it, though.

Illus. 57 (below). Attach the stem and flower to the candle in an attractive position.

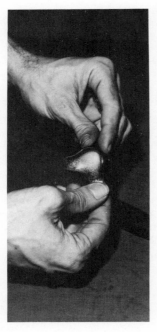

Illus. 55. Pull another edge upwards in the same manner.

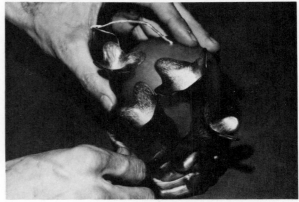

MUSHROOMS

Making mushroom caps from dipped tapers is not as difficult as it looks, and the result is an entirely different candle. Hand-form a mushroom body—you needn't be too scrupulous about this; a rough cylinder with a slightly wider and flattened base is fine. Dip it into hot wax a few times to cover it with color. Now slice off both ends of a dipped taper. With your thumb, peel the outer color layer away from the middle of the taper (Illus. 58). Don't squeeze the rest of the taper as you peel the wax back. When you have

the cylinder until you have 4 or 5 petals (Illus. 56). Take the flower and press it onto the candle. Use melted wax to attach it if necessary. Twist the stem round the candle and press it on. Take care not to

peeled the wax away from half of the taper, try pushing the middle from the other end. With a little effort, you can remove the middle and separate it from the outside layer (Illus. 59). If the center won't come out, peel back a little more of the outside layer.

Gently pull the wax on one side until the color layer takes the shape of a mushroom cap (Illus. 60). Punch a hole for the wick and place the cap over the top of the mushroom body. Squeeze the edges down round the wick (Illus. 61). Press the wax firmly round the

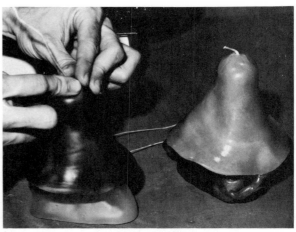

Illus. 61. Press the wax round the wick.

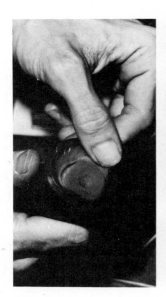

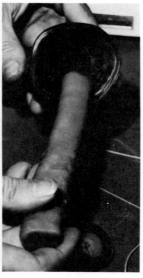

Illus. 58. Peel the outer layer of wax away from a warm taper.

Illus. 59 . Push the middle of the taper out of the outer layer.

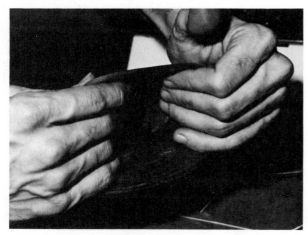

Illus. 60. Gently widen the outer layer.

body of the mushroom and, once the cap has the right shape, immerse it in water for a few seconds to harden it. Cut off small pieces from the center piece and form them into vines. Place these around the body of the mushroom. Finish the entire mushroom with hot wax.

COOKIE CUTTER APPLIQUÉS

Cookie cutters (which are available in a wide variety of sizes and shapes) open up many possibilities for appliqué design. Try making a flower design. You'll need some small, flower-shaped cookie cutters, a cake pan, sequin pins, and some ribbon (ribbon is an added touch—you can leave it out if you wish).

First make a hurricane candle. (Since ribbon and sequin pins are used for this candle, a hurricane candle is used. However, the basic process is applicable to any type of candle.) Spray the cake pan with mould release and pour about $\frac{1}{8}$ inch of dyed, 135° F. (57° C.) melting point wax into it. When it is almost cool, cut small flowers out with the cookie cutter, and then pop the whole sheet of wax out. Now spray in more mould release and pour in a different color of wax (for leaves for the flowers). Let it cool, cut out the leaf shapes with an appropriate cookie cutter (Illus. 62), and pop out the sheet of wax.

Heat the flowers and leaves under a heat lamp or in the oven wrapped in a towel at the lowest temperature until they are soft. Melt a can of dyed wax (for the middles of the flowers) and a can of microcrystalline wax, or 135° F. (57° C.) melting point wax, for use as an adhesive.

Hold the flower shapes in your hand and gently push it down around your finger until the edges curve upward (Illus. 63).

Place the leaves behind the flowers so that they stick out on either side (Illus. 64). Gently squeeze the flower and the leaves together. Now dip the paintbrush into the can of dyed wax and place a small

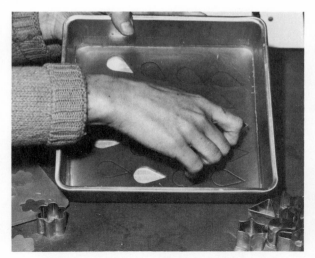

Illus. 62. Pull the leaf shapes out of the wax.

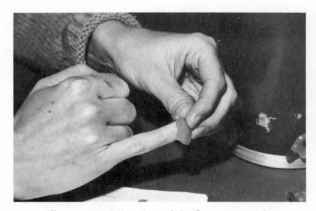

Illus. 63. Bend the edges of the flowers upwards.

Illus. 64. You may need to use hot wax to attach the leaves to the flowers.

and on the appropriate spot on the shell (Illus. 67). Firmly hold the flower on that spot until it adheres—a few seconds should do (Illus. 68). Place all the flowers on the hurricane shell in this manner.

Attach a ribbon to the top of the hurricane shell with sequin pins (Illus. 69). The candle is finished and ready for burning.

Illus. 65 (left). Brush a little hot wax (of a different color) on the center of each flower. Illus. 66 (right). Brush some more hot wax (undyed wax this time) on the back of the flower.

center on the flower (Illus. 65). Repeat this process until you have enough flowers for the hurricane shell.

Attach the ribbon round the base of the shell with sequin pins. Take care not to crack the wax. Now place some hot wax on the back of a flower (Illus. 66)

Illus. 67. Hot wax binds the flower to the shell.

Illus. 68 (above). Remember not to press down too hard on the shell.

Illus. 69. Ribbon sets off the flowers on the shell very nicely.

Appliqué with Other Materials

There are an endless number of appliqué materials to choose from. Craft shops have many gold and silver patterns made especially for candles (Illus. 70). Glitter sequins, gift wrapping paper, pieces of old costume jewelry, paper flowers and pieces of cloth all look good when cut and arranged into pleasing designs on your candle. Just cut and apply anything that comes to mind. You can always remove what you don't like. Attach the appliqué pieces with sequin pins, white glue, or hot wax. Finish them with hot wax.

Illus. 70. Gold and silver paper patterns, thoughtfully placed, enhance any candle very nicely, and are available at most craft shops.

6

Water Candles

Water candles are quite different from any other type of candle. They are basically elaborate wax shapes with a replaceable block candle in the middle. It might take a little practice at first to master the techniques, but the results are well worth it. And best of all, water candles, like hurricane candles, last forever. Try making a few—with a candle burning inside, these fanciful and airy castles of wax are truly a pleasure to look upon.

To make the water candle you need a large container, such as a plastic garbage can, 6 pounds of 145° F. (63° C.) melting point wax, 10 ounces of plastic additive (if you make a larger or smaller candle, the proportions are about 1 part plastic additive to 9 parts wax), one 8- or 9-inch pie tin (dish), and a 2- or 3-inch-diameter block candle (for the candle in the middle).

Fill the large container to within 8 inches of the top with cold water. Heat the wax to a temperature of 215° F. (102° C.) and add the plastic additive. Stir until all the plastic additive has dissolved and then let the wax cool until it reaches a temperature of about 165° F. (74° C.).

Place the block candle in the middle of the pie tin and pour the melted wax into the tin until it is level with the lip. Let this cool until there is a thick crust of hard wax over the top. Now place the pie tin and candle into cold water so it will harden quickly.

When the wax in the pie tin is cold (Illus. 71), pop the candle and base out. Fill a pouring container (such as a coffee pot) with the wax heated earlier. Make sure the wax is heated to 165° F. (74° C.). Place the base candle in the container at an angle of 30 degrees to the water, so the edge of the circular base is the only part touching the water. Pour the wax along the edge of the base (Illus. 72). Pour it directly onto the base, *not* into the water. Pour just enough wax to form a half circle about 2 inches out from the base. If you pour too much, or the wax flows over the water too quickly, fold the wax back onto itself (Illus. 73). Let the wax cool for a moment in this position, and then repeat the procedure on another side of the base. Make four or five semi-circles round the edge of the base (Illus. 74).

After you have made all the semi-circles, push the candle into the water, this time keeping it straight, until the water just covers the base. The edges of the semi-circles should protrude from the water at a 30-degree angle.

Illus. 71 (right). When this base candle burns out, just replace it with another.

Illus. 72 (below). Pour the wax onto the edge of the base.

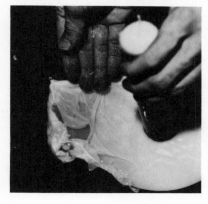

Illus. 73. If the wax spreads out too much, fold it back.

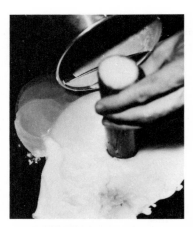

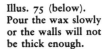

Illus. 74. Don't pour too much wax onto the base.

Illus. 75 (below). Pour the wax slowly or the walls will not be thick enough.

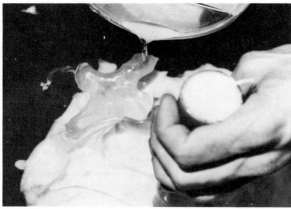

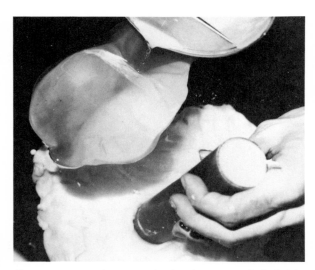

Illus. 76. Immerse the candle slowly when you reach the height of the base candle.

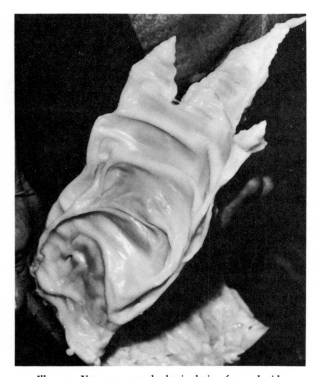

Illus. 77. You can vary the basic design for each side.

Now, pour the wax slowly back and forth along the inside of one of the semi-circles and, at the same time, push the base candle slowly down into the water (Illus. 75). Take your time with this—the longer you take to push the candle into the water, the thicker the sides of the wax shell.

You can see a column of wax taking shape, extending down into the water, as you push the candle down. If you pour too fast, the pool of molten wax on top of the water will spread out. If this happens, just fold the wax back onto itself until the pool is the right size. Then begin pouring and submerging again.

When you reach the height of the base candle, stop pouring and decrease the speed with which you immerse the candle (Illus. 76). Reach under the sides of the molten pool of wax and pinch one or two sections together to form two or three pools. Begin immersing the candle again but this time do it in smooth, quick spurts. You will see small spires begin to take shape. When you come near the end of the spire, push the candle down about ½ inch and then lift it back very quickly and hold the section out of water for a few seconds. Then repeat the procedure. This produces small, shell-like forms. When the spires are long enough, pinch off the ends and hold the entire candle in the water for a few minutes. Then just let it float for five minutes or so. This should harden the wax sufficiently (Illus. 77).

Hold the candle in the water just as you did for the first semi-circle. Pour the wax along the semi-circle next to the side you just finished. Try to attach this pool of wax to the finished side. Move it with your hand if you have to. Pour and immerse just as you did for the first side. You can separate this side from the finished side and rejoin the sides at a higher point, if you wish.

Make the spires according to the procedure detailed earlier. Repeat this process for each side. Make sure the candle cools between each pouring.

Remember that the slower you immerse the candle, the thicker the sides. You may find that it requires two people to make a water candle—one to push the candle into the water and the other to pour the wax. If your first try isn't successful, just melt down the wax and try again. Don't worry about water in the wax—it just sinks to the bottom of the container.

There are several ways to color the water candle: you can dye the wax that you pour; you can pour small amounts of colored wax into the pools of wax as you push the candle into the water; or, you can sprinkle small amounts of powdered dye onto the sides of the wax walls and melt it over the wax with a torch.

You can also use a torch to melt contours and holes in the sides, attach additional pieces, and repair areas of the water candle that accidentally break.

When the middle candle burns out, just replace it with another. With proper care, your beautiful water candle can last for years and years.

7

Painted and Whipped-Wax Candles

Painting Candles

Although not all candles are improved by painting, the beauty of some types or designs is greatly enhanced and strengthened by the thoughtful use of dyed wax or dye. Hand-formed shapes and the more basic moulded candles, for instance, quite often benefit from some added color and texture. There are several different ways to paint your candles, so choose whichever you think will do more for your candle.

PAINTING WITH WAX

Painting wax on wax creates a texture and appearance that is totally unique. You can make humorous and whimsical animals, people, and plants, and transform ordinary block candles into wildly original creations.

The only materials you need are microcrystalline wax, a number of small cans, and a few $1\frac{1}{2}$-inch brushes.

First, either hand-form an interesting shape (Illus. 78), or make a suitable candle in a mould. After the candle has hardened, melt several cans of microcrystalline wax. Melt one can for each color you intend to use. You do not need to heat the wax much past its melting point. Add your dyes after the wax melts. Use a larger than usual quantity of dye so you won't need to paint more than a few coats.

Dip the brush into the microcrystalline wax and brush a little on the candle (Illus. 79). Try it a few more times. Let the brush cool for a minute until it is just beginning to get stiff and then briskly brush back and forth over the painted area. This causes the wax to build up and form a textured surface. Add other colors and form a textured surface over the entire candle (Illus. 80). Now, with a small amount of another color, brush lightly and briskly over the entire surface. This highlights the texture and adds more color to the candle.

If your candle requires eyes, take two beads and attach them in appropriate spots with short, large-headed nails.

There is really nothing more to these candles than that. Try making one—you'll be surprised at how

Illus. 78. When you hand-form a shape, don't worry about surface imperfections—the wax will cover them.

Illus. 79. Brush some liquid wax on the candle.

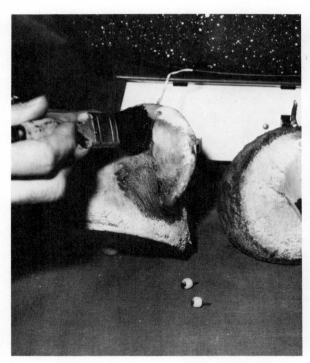

Illus. 80. Add as many colors as you wish. Texture each new area of color before you add the next.

Illus. 81. Move the melting dye around the candle.

easy it is. Just make sure you don't over-paint. If you apply too many layers of wax the texture becomes very bumpy. If this is the case, or if you simply don't like the candle, just scrape the wax off with a knife and start over.

If you want a smooth painted finish on your candle, use 135° F. (57° C.) melting point wax instead of microcrystalline wax. However, this wax does not give a texture.

PAINTING WITH DYE

Applying color with a torch is a simple way to create unique effects. Make any type of candle, but do not dye it. Place the finished candle on its side and sprinkle a small amount of dye on a part of it Now light your propane torch and adjust it to a very low flame. Run the flame over the area covered with dye (Illus. 81). Make the motion smooth and fast. Do it again if you want to move the color around. The dye melts into the wax and forms interesting, vivid patches of color.

Sprinkle a small amount of another dye next to the first area and repeat the process. If you get too much color in a given area, just scrape some off with a knife. Continue adding colors until the entire candle is covered with dye and you are satisfied with the effect. For an added touch, rub on a small amount of gold or silver paint in areas between the dyes. You can run the torch over the paint or leave it as is.

Whipped-Wax Candles

Whipped wax is available commercially, but is expensive and takes many hours to dry. However, there is an alternative—you can make it yourself. The

only special materials you need are a bowl and an eggbeater.

Pour any melting point wax into a bowl, add some stearic acid, and beat it just like you would an egg. Beat it until the wax becomes frothy, like whipped cream. Then, before it begins to cool, apply it to any candle with a knife or spatula (Illus. 82). If you wish to dye the wax, add the dye to the wax just before you beat it. If you want the wax to be white, add only stearic acid.

Many different candles can be decorated with whipped wax. You can make your own snowmen, snowballs, bases for moulded candles, Christmas trees, and even imitation ice-cream sundaes!

8

Moulds, Wicks and Dyes

A good understanding of the materials used in candle-making is almost essential, even for a casual candle-maker. There are a great number of products to choose from, each with its own particular uses and limitations. Beautiful, professional-looking candles require a knowledge of each material that goes into the candle. For instance, unless you know the right type of wick to use for a given candle, the candle might melt too quickly, or drip excessively, or smoke.

Unless you know the materials it is almost impossible, or at least time-consuming and expensive, to experiment or try to create new types of candles—and that's half the fun of candle-making.

Moulds

Moulds are available in all shapes and sizes. They are available from craft shops and are made from metal, rubber, or plastic. The metal moulds come in a wide variety of designs—balls, squares, stars, half-moons, and many more. All metal moulds are very durable and, with proper care, can last quite a while. Metal moulds are slightly tapered at the bottom so the candle can be easily removed. They come equipped with a wick sealing screw for the bottom wick hole. A point to remember with these, and all other types of moulds, is that the bottom of the mould is always the top of the candle.

Plastic moulds are available in many more shapes than the metal moulds. Since many of the moulds consist of two halves, more intricate (and sometimes odder) designs are possible. The two-piece moulds are held together with small metal clamps. Try not to pour them with wax heated to temperatures higher than 190° F. (88° C.)—they will often leak if you do. If you find that your plastic mould leaks regardless of the temperature of the wax you pour into it, use larger, stronger clamps and, instead of using the wood stands provided with the mould to hold the mould in place, put masking tape along the bottom of the mould and place it firmly in damp sand.

Rubber moulds are usually one-piece, glove-like moulds. They are hung downward when filled with wax and peeled off like a glove when cool. Rubber moulds are easily handled and withstand much abuse. There are a few problems with them however. Sometimes the moulds distort from wax shrinkage and the water pressure in the water bath. If this happens to your rubber moulds, try air-cooling them. String the wick with an embroidery needle. Now cut a hole in a cardboard box just large enough for the mould to fit into but not large enough for the small lip of the mould. Place the mould in the hole and push some small nails through the lip of the mould into the cardboard. This secures the mould and prevents excessive distortion.

When it is time to remove the rubber mould from the hardened candle, either sprinkle some talc on the outside of the mould or place some vegetable oil on it. By doing this, you allow the rubber to pull against itself. Otherwise it tends to stick and might get ripped when being pulled off.

Plexiglas acrylic moulds are slightly tapered, seamless moulds which require no water bath and can be safely handled when filled with hot wax without danger of burning your hands. They do not require a mould release, and they enable the candle maker to pour at 200° F. (93° C.) safely without distortion of the mould. When embedding flowers, leaves or other objects, the transparent mould will permit checking that the detail is correct before pouring.

You can find many types of moulds around the house. Jello moulds, cottage cheese containers, cups, bowls, paper cups, glasses, and tin cans without lips all work well. You can use almost anything as long as it won't break from the heat of the hot wax. Just be sure that you can remove the finished candle from it when cool.

To place the wick in a home-made mould, drill a hole through the candle. (If you drill completely through the wax, just take some soft wax and plug it up.) Pour the hole full of hot wax and immediately place a suitable wick into it. You can also make the wick hole by heating an ice pick or coathanger and melting a hole through the wax. This does not work as nicely as the drilling does though.

You can make your own moulds from plaster or rubber. Make the form for your mould out of wax (see the section on hand-forming starting on page 14), and shape it by using the torch. Use silk to shape and polish any fragile areas. Dip the form into hot wax to give it a smooth finish.

Plaster is a good material to use if you are going to make a large mould—it is inexpensive and is easily repaired if it becomes chipped or cracked. Soak the plaster mould in water for a few hours prior to pouring. This prevents the wax from being absorbed into the plaster and also aids in the cooling process.

Rubber mould-making material is also available in some craft shops. This rubber is a silicone rubber that vulcanizes (hardens) at toom temperature. The rubber is mixed together and poured or painted over a wax form. It hardens overnight into a glove-like, stretchable, durable mould. If you want a wick hole in your mould, just push a nail into the top of the wax shape and pour the rubber over it. When the rubber is hard, cut the rubber round the top of the nail and remove it before you pull the rubber off the wax form. It is advisable to first coat a flat board with wax, then place the wax form on it, before pouring the rubber.

PROPER CARE OF YOUR MOULDS

Metal moulds scratch and dent easily. Take care not to drop or scratch them. If you have to scrape wax from the inside of the mould, use a wooden instrument. Once a metal mould has been dented, the candle is hard to remove, and if it is scratched, the candle will show the marks.

Keep all your moulds clean. You can use hot, soapy water to clean most moulds. Rinse the mould with clean, hot water, then dry, before you use or store it. When your moulds are not in use, set them out of the way, up-side-down, to prevent dust and dirt from accumulating in them. With proper care, your moulds can last indefinitely.

WICK SEALERS

There are several ways to seal the wick hole in the bottom of the mould: with wick sealing screws; with florists' putty; with mould sealing putty; with masking tape; and with damp sand. The wick sealing screws are just sheet metal screws and they do not always seal properly. Florists' putty is very good but you must place the mould into the water bath fairly quickly, as the putty gets soft and sometimes falls off when it is heated by the hot wax. The same holds true of mould sealing putty, which is very similar but not so sticky. Damp sand functions well for two-piece moulds and in combination with one of the other methods. To ensure that the wick hole doesn't leak, combine methods. Place florists' putty over the wick screw or, if you use only florists' putty, place your mould in damp sand. Or, you can place tape over the wick screw or over the putty. Florists' putty is available in any florists' shop and is more economical than the wick sealing putty sold in craft shops.

MOULD RELEASE

The most effective and widely used mould release is silicone spray mould release. There are many brand names on the market, but all of them work equally well. Silicone spray mould release is available at some craft shops and is essential for most moulded candles. A thin coating on the inside of the mould is sufficient, but if you want to give your candle a textured surface, use more.

Wicks

When you light the wick the flame melts the surrounding wax. Because of the porous nature of the wick the molten wax is absorbed and travels up the wick, where it is burned off. The flame is constantly fed fuel in this manner and the wax is slowly consumed.

When you choose the wick for your candle, certain factors must be taken into consideration: the melting point of the wax; the size of the candle; and the purpose of the candle. The size of the hole melted in the candle is directly related to the size of the wick and the melting point temperature of the wax. Just about any wick will work for a candle as long as it is not obviously too large or too small. If the wick is too small, it will not consume much wax and, as a result, the molten pool will increase until it flows over the sides of the candle. Also, if the wick is too small, and the melting point of the wax is too high, there will not be enough heat to melt the wax and the candle will go out. On the other hand, a wick that is too large will burn quickly and smoke excessively and will have too large a flame.

Think about the purpose of the candle when you choose the wick size. Do you want a dripless candle (dripless candles cannot have a diameter larger than about $1\frac{1}{2}$ inches and still be completely consumed by the flame), a candle with sides that spread out, or a glow-through candle? In the case of the dripless candle, the function of the wick is to consume all the wax. The flame should be medium size and should burn without smoking. So, since the diameter of the candle is small, use a fairly small wick. To make a candle that drips, just increase the size of the wick or decrease the melting point of the wax.

For a candle with sides that spread out the wick has to melt the wax within $\frac{1}{4}$ inch of the outside of the candle. The thin wax shell that is left will curl und bend down the outside of the candle. Use your own good judgment and keep experimenting until you get the effect that you're after. Remember, the larger the wick and the lower the melting point, the larger the hole melted in the candle.

If you want a candle to have a glow-through effect, use 145° F. (63° C.) melting point wax and a medium-size wick (for a medium-size candle.) A well or hole will melt down into the candle as it burns. You can refill the hole after it burns to the bottom, or place a small candle into it.

As a starting point, use a 24-ply wick for taper candles, a 30-ply wick for 2 to 4 inch (diameter) candles, and a 36-ply wick for candles larger than 4 inches. If you use a wire core wick, ask for a comparable size. Try a larger size if the candle goes out, and a smaller size if the candle smokes too much.

Wire core wick is made by braiding prepared cotton round a metal core. As the wick burns, the metal melts into very small droplets and rests in the molten pool of wax. Wire core wick works well in any type of candle, but is especially useful when making candles that require that the wick be put in after the wax has been poured. It is a good wick to use when you want a uniform hole melted in your candle.

Flat braided wick is an unbleached, prepared wick. It is made from cotton and is braided into three strands. Each wick has a certain number of threads, or, as they are usually called, plies. The greater the number of plies, the thicker the wick. Flat braided wick is available in a wide range of sizes: 15-ply, 21-ply, 24-ply, 30-ply, 36-ply, 42-ply, 48-ply, and 60-ply. The 15-ply has 15 threads, the 30-ply has 30 threads, and so on. Flat braided wick is difficult to thread through the wick holes and, as it burns, it tends to droop over and extinguish the flame. Before you string it through the wick hole, give it a few coats of wax heated to 170° F. (77° C.) for added stiffness.

Square braided wick is a bleached, prepared wick having four sides. It is also made up of plies, but it is not designated by the number of strands or plies. As with the wire core wick, each manufacturer has his own code numbers for sizes. It is available in a full range of sizes, and is better for large candles than the flat braided wick due to its stiffness. It is easy to string and will not bend over as it burns. As with the flat braided wick, it is suggested that you coat it with hot wax a few times to increase the stiffness.

The type of wick you use really depends on the type of candle you are making and the type of wick that you have on hand. Any type of wick will work in any candle, but certain wicks function better in certain candles. If the wick you have on hand is too small, just twist two or three of them together and dip them into hot wax a few times.

HOME-MADE WICKS

If commercial wick is not available, cotton string, or even clothes line, if you are making very large candles, will work. However, you must treat any material besides commercial wick in a chemical solution to ensure smokeless, even burning.

Make the solution from 2 tablespoons of table salt, 4 tablespoons of borax, and two cups of water. Soak the cotton string in this solution for 8 hours. Let the string dry, either in the air or in the oven at a low heat. When all the moisture is gone, coat the string with wax.

PREPARATION OF WICKS

Prior to placing the wick in the mould or candle, it is best to coat it with wax. This will stiffen the wick and facilitate stringing through the wick hole. Coating cotton wicks also eliminates any air trapped between the fibres. Dip the wick into hot wax, let it cool a few seconds, and dip it again. Apply four coats of wax in this way. Set it aside and let it cool completely. If you want to coat a whole spool of wick (or a similarly large quantity) at once, place it in a container of wax heated to 170° F. (77° C.). The melting point of the wax makes no difference. Make sure the wick is not touching the bottom of the container or it will scorch. Leave the spool of wick in the heated wax (in the double boiler) for 3 to 5 hours. Remove the spool and let it cool on a clean surface. The wick will peel off easily and no further preparation is needed.

Dyes

Color is an important part of any candle. With the proper use of dyes, soft, pastel shades or rich, vibrant tones are possible. If used in the wrong way, you'll get dark, muddy colors. There are two types of coloring. One is pigment and the other is dye. Pigments do not go into solution, they go into suspension. In other words, they form small particles that float or hang in the liquid wax. As long as you stir the wax occasionally, these small particles give the appearance of color, but they soon settle to the bottom of the mould or heating container. If pigment is used to color wax, the finished candle will be darker at the bottom.

Dyes fall into two categories—oil soluble and water soluble. Because wax is a petroleum by-product, oil-soluble dyes are the only type you can use. These dyes are not like pigments; they do not go into suspension, they go into solution. That is, they actually become part of the wax. If dyes are properly dispersed throughout the wax they will never settle and your candles will have uniform color. Dyes are available in both powdered and solid form. The solid dyes are nothing more than powdered dyes that have been mixed with stearic acid and cooled.

Experiment with your dyes. The colors are often deceptive in liquid wax. Red especially appears lighter in liquid wax than in solid, so don't add too much. The color will come out as the wax hardens.

The only dyes you really need are red, yellow and blue. Add red to blue to obtain purple; a small amount of red added to yellow produces orange; and yellow and blue mixed together yield green. Decrease or increase the proportions of each color in a mixture to obtain lighter or darker shades.

The only problem with dyes is that they sometimes fade if left for extended periods in the sun or under fluorescent lighting. If you are careful and keep your candles away from these two sources of light, the color will remain bright. Some wax refineries are now putting small amounts of anti-oxidants into their waxes to prevent oxidation and the yellowing of the wax, but it is best to use precautions.

Crayons are sometimes used to dye wax. However, it is not a good idea to use them for dyeing as they are made from plastic. The plastic does not disperse well and when it burns, it collects around the wick in the form of carbon. You should also be cautious when using fluorescent dyes. They do not disperse well, and usually sink to the bottom of the heating container. If they remain on the bottom of the container for any length of time, they scorch and form an insoluble mass. They do not burn well and, in most cases, they actually put out the candle flame by forming large carbon deposits. Fluorescent dyes also fade quickly. You can use them, though, in certain instances. They will disperse well if you use them for whipped wax, and small amounts added to regular dyes help to brighten the colors.

9

Waxes and Additives

Wax

Wax is a petroleum by-product. It is obtained by the distillation and "cracking" of crude oil. Distillation of crude oil results in the physical separation of its hydrocarbon components according to their boiling points. Cracking is the breaking of the hydrocarbon molecule to produce new products.

In the distillation process, a segment or "cut" is obtained for the manufacture of lubricating oils. This cut is processed mainly by solvent refining. "Dewaxing" of these oils is the source of petroleum waxes.

There are two basic types of petroleum waxes used in candle-making: paraffin (macrocrystalline) and microcrystalline. Paraffin waxes have melting points of up to 140° F. (60° C.). The microcrystalline waxes have melting points ranging from 140° F. (60° C.) to over 200° F. (93° C.). Some of these microcrystalline waxes are soft and pliable while others are hard and brittle.

There is a pronounced difference between paraffin and microcrystalline wax. Paraffin wax has large, well-formed crystals, while microcrystalline wax, as the name implies, has small, irregular crystals. Even though there is an overlap in the melting point of these waxes, the microcrystalline waxes differ in chemical composition and physical properties. In candle-making, they are used to increase layer adhesion, hardness and flexibility, and for sculpting and painting.

Waxes are designated by the temperature at which they melt, or melting point. Each melting point has its own characteristics. The most commonly used waxes in candle-making range from very soft 128° F. (53° C.) melting point wax to fairly hard 165° F. (74° C.) melting point wax. In this wide range there is a suitable wax for every candle-making purpose.

The lower melting point waxes tend to be very soft and oily. They are easily shaped when warm. They are also very ductile, so you can stretch them into interesting shapes for appliqués. They release from the mould fairly easily, but the finished candle is easily marred by handling and adversely affected by warm weather.

Higher melting point, or intermediate, waxes are more brittle and cannot be hand-formed. On the other hand, they release from the mould very well and are less oily. They produce candles that are resistant to handling and stand up well in warm weather. These waxes are best suited for block candles, base candles for appliqués, and sand-cast candles. You can alter their properties by blending in lower melting point waxes, microcrystalline waxes, stearic acid, or plastic additives.

CANDLE WAX CHARACTERISTICS

Every wax varies according to its melting point. Take into consideration properties such as elongation, melting point, and hardness when making a candle. Elongation or ductility is the ability of the wax to stretch without breaking. Hardness is usually related to melting point—the lower melting points are generally soft and the higher melting points hard. The exception to this rule is found in certain microcrystalline waxes which are soft and workable even though they have high melting points.

128° F. (53° C.): This is a soft, ductile wax with good translucency. It colors well and has fair mould-release qualities. Due to its low melting point, the finished candle is easily marred by handling, and if the candle has a small diameter it tends to droop or sag in hot weather. It is best suited for filling container candles, making hand-formed appliqués, and blending.

135° F. (57° C.): This wax gives a better finish than the 128° F. melting point wax. It is moderately resistant to hot weather and has a fairly hard finish. Because it is ductile, it is well-suited to hand-formed appliqués and for blending. It is also used for taper candles. This wax takes color well and has good mould-release properties.

145° F. (63° C.): This is one of the most useful candle waxes. It takes color well and has good mould-release properties. It gives a smooth hard finish, is resistant to hot weather, and is fairly transparent. It is used for block candles, sand-cast candles, water candles, and bases for appliqué candles, and is sometimes used as the base for a blend.

150°–160° F. (66°–71° C.) (there is actually more than one wax in this melting range point, but they all have basically the same uses): This is hard, oil-free wax. It gives a smooth, glossy finish, is slightly opaque, takes color well, and has very good mould-release properties. Use it as a base for a blend or as a glaze wax. This wax (and all higher melting point waxes) are not recommended for candles. Unless blended, a candle made from this wax alone might fracture.

165° F. (74° C.): This is also a hard wax with good mould-release properties. It is used as a blend to increase the hardness of lower melting point waxes.

Danish Taper Wax: This is a hard candle wax with many additives designed to make the thin Danish taper. It is very opaque, colors well, gives a smooth, hard finish, and picks up mould detail well. It is quite resistant to hot weather, but is very brittle. The mould-release properties are good.

Scale Wax: This is a general-purpose, unrefined, very oily wax. Due to the amount of oil it contains, it will cause mottling when moulded into any candle shape. For this reason, you can use it for mottled candles, but it is not recommended for any other purpose except for container candles. The reason it is sometimes used for these candles is its low cost.

Microcrystalline Wax: This wax has melting points from 140°–200° F. (60°–93° C.). It can be pliable and tacky or hard and brittle. It has poor mould-release qualities when used alone. Because it is easily shaped and sticks to itself, it is often used for appliqués. When blended with regular candle waxes, it reduces brittleness and fracturing, eliminates mottling and pitting, and prevents layer separation. It takes dye well, and is very translucent when blended. It also increases the ductibility and stickiness of the lower melting point waxes, and a blend of the two waxes is excellent for use in hand-forming. The suggested proportions for a good blend are 1 part microcrystalline wax to 9 parts of the other wax. Increase or decrease these proportions to meet your individual requirements.

Shaping Wax: This is a blend of refined and microcrystalline wax sold in some craft shops. It has fair mould-release qualities, good translucency, and takes color well. You can use it for appliqués and hand-forming. This blend produces a rough, rather unique texture when painted on a candle. You can usually substitute this wax for microcrystalline wax if the latter is not available.

Beeswax: This wax is very costly and has a high melting point. It is long-burning, smokeless, and has poor mould-release qualities. Mix it half and half with any refined candle wax when making block candles. If a mould release problem occurs, add 1 part stearic acid to 9 parts wax. Beeswax is usually available in sheets from craft shops. You can just wrap the sheets round a wick to form a beeswax taper candle (see page 16).

WAX STORAGE

Wax storage presents few problems. Just store the wax in a cool place and keep it covered so no dirt or dust can collect on it. Before melting your wax to make candles, check the slabs for dirt and moisture.

Nothing destroys the appearance of a finished candle more than suspended dirt caused by careless storage.

Blending Waxes

If a certain melting point wax is unavailable, or if you wish to combine the characteristics of two waxes or if one of your waxes proves hard to work with, you may want to try blending.

Blending two or more waxes together will usually give you an average of their individual characteristics. For instance, if you blend equal proportions of 128° F. (53° C.) melting point wax and 145° F. (63° C.) melting point wax, the resulting wax will have more or less the same characteristics and melting point as 135° F. (57° C.) melting point wax. Or, to take another instance, if you blend microcrystalline wax with a low melting point wax, the wax that is produced will be stickier and better suited for hand-forming and appliqués.

If you decide you need to make a blend, just go through the list of waxes until you find one with the characteristics you wish your base wax to have. Add this wax to your base wax until you get the right combination. The best way to do this is to make several batches at once—each of a different proportion—and then, after the wax has hardened, choose the best blend. It's a good idea to keep a record of these experimental batches—that is, their proportions and characteristics—just in case you need to make a blend of the same waxes at some later date.

Additives

Mottling Oil: This is a clear petroleum by-product available in craft shops. Use ordinary mineral oil as a substitute if you can't find mottling oil.

Scents: There are many scents available in craft shops. They vary a great deal in effectiveness and, as a result, the amount needed to scent a pound of wax varies. Just experiment with them.

Plastic Additive: Plastic additives are sold under a variety of trade names. These additives increase the color, gloss, and hardness of candles. Use 1 to 2 teaspoons of additive per pound of wax. Use larger amounts to make water candles.

Stearic Acid: This is a mild, non-corrosive, low melting point, organic acid. There is no danger in handling it. It should be stored in a cool, dry area. It is a hard, white, glossy material, made up of small chips, and having an odor similar to tallow. Stearic acid is sold in all craft shops that sell candle-making equipment. Stearic acid is essential in candle-making. It helps mould release, brightens colors, strengthens waxes, and gives a smooth, glossy finish. Use approximately 3 tablespoons of stearic acid per 1 pound of wax for most candles. This is not a fixed proportion, so experiment with it if you wish. Use more stearic acid with a low melting point wax or when you want your candle to be perfectly white.

Trouble-Shooting

While gaining experience as a candle-maker, you may run into various problems or find that an unduly large number of your candles have imperfections. Almost all of these problems have simple solutions.

Bubbles at the base of the candle: The water level in the water bath was too low. The water level must be even with or above the level of wax in the mould.

Candle smokes: The wick is too large and the melting point of wax is too low; the air pocket resulting from wax shrinkage was not completely filled; or the candle is burning in a draft.

Fractures (thermal cracks): The candle cooled too rapidly; the water was too cold; or the candle cooled in a draft of cold air. Fractures also appear when the air pocket caused by shrinkage is filled with wax heated to temperatures above 195° F. (91° C.).

Frost Marks: The wax was poured at too low a temperature; wax particles from a previous candle were left in the mould; the mould itself was too cold when the wax was poured into it; the wax was poured at too high a temperature; or too much stearic acid or plastic additive was added to the wax.

Layer Separation (in layer candles): The wax was poured at too low a temperature; one or more of the layers were allowed to cool for too long.

Mottling: The wax cooled too slowly, allowing large crystals to form near the edges of the candle. Add a small amount of microcrystalline wax or plastic additive (1 part to 50 parts wax), and cool the candle a little faster.

Pit marks: The mould was not left in the water long enough; or too much mould release was used.

Pock marks: The wax was poured at too high a temperature.

Water in candle: The mould wasn't sealed well enough before you placed it in the water bath; or water found its way into the wax before it was poured into the mould.

Glossary

Appliqué candle: An appliqué candle is a candle with either a hand-formed or moulded piece of wax or a non-wax object attached for decoration.

Base candle: A base candle is a moulded or hand-formed candle on which a more elaborate candle is built.

Block candle: A block candle is any candle made with a mould.

Container candle: A container candle is a candle which has been formed in a container of some sort, usually a glass, and not removed.

Danish taper: Danish tapers are long, thin, curved candles, dipped like tapers, but with many additives in the wax.

Dip tank: The dip tank is any large container, filled with either hot wax or cold water, into which the candle is dipped.

Dye chips: Dye chips are pieces of solid candle dye.

Florists' putty: Florists' putty, available in florists' shops, is used to seal the wick hole in candle moulds.

Flower fantasy candle: The flower fantasy candle is a candle with plastic flowers or plants embedded in the wax.

Glow-through candle: A glow-through candle is any candle with an unmelted outer shell, through which the light glows.

Hand-formed candle: A hand-formed candle is any candle shaped without a mould.

Hurricane candle: A hurricane candle is an outer wax shell with a small votive candle inside. The name comes from their ability to stay lit when exposed to the wind.

Melting point: Melting point is temperature at which a wax melts. It is used to designate the various waxes.

Microcrystalline wax: Microcrystalline wax has high melting points and can be either pliable and tacky or hard and brittle. Melting points from 140° F. (60° C.) to 170° F. (77° C.) are used in candle-making, usually in combination with another wax for painting.

Mottling: Mottling is the forming of snowflake-like crystals in the wax. It is caused by the addition of mottling oil or mineral oil.

Mould release: Mould release is a silicone spray or rinse used to assist the removal of the hardened candle wax from the mould. When used in reference to waxes, it denotes the ability to release from the mould.

Moulds: A mould is any form used to shape the wax.

Mould sealer: Mould sealer is used to seal the wick hole in candle moulds. It is more expensive but basically the same as florists' putty.

Paraffin: The term paraffin is used to designate the group of refined waxes with melting points as high as 190° F. (92° C.).

Plastic additive: Plastic additive is used to harden waxes, brighten colors, and increase gloss. One type makes the candle more opaque; the other makes it a little more translucent.

Sand-casting: Sand-casting is the process of forming a candle using sand as a mould. Candles formed in this manner may or may not have sand crusts.

Sculpting wax: Sculpting wax is a name that microcrystalline wax, or a blend of microcrystalline wax and refined wax, is sold by in some craft shops.

Seam line: The seam line is the line on a finished block candle formed by the impression of the seam in the mould.

Shaping wax: Shaping wax is another blend of microcrystalline wax and refined wax.

Stearic acid: Stearic acid is a mild, non-corrosive acid made from animal fats and used in almost all candles to brighten colors, strengthen the wax, and improve the mould release and finish. Its chemical formula is $CH(CH)COOH$.

Votive candles: Votive candles are small, simple candles, usually, but not necessarily in glass containers. They originated as religious candles.

Water bath: A water bath refers to a bucket of water into which the filled metal candle mould is placed to cool.

Water candle: A water candle is a candle which is, basically, moulded by water pressure and the speed with which the water cools the wax.

Wax shrinkage: All waxes expand with heat and contract as they cool. Wax shrinkage occurs in all candles.

Whipped wax: Whipped wax is wax that has been beaten into a froth. It is available in craft shops, but can be made at home.

Wick sealing screw: The wick sealing screw is a small metal screw provided with candle moulds that is used to seal wick holes.

Index